EXPLORE OUR WORLD

SECOND EDITION • WORKBOOK

Unit 0 2
Unit 1 My School 5
Unit 2 My Toys 9
Unit 3 My Family 13
Unit 4 My Body 17
Units 1-4 Review 21
Unit 5 Stories 23
Unit 6 I Like Food 27
Unit 7 Clothes 31
Unit 8 Animals 35
Units 5-8 Review 39
Writing 41
Cutouts 57

NATIONAL GEOGRAPHIC LEARNING

Australia • Brazil • Mexico • Singapore • United Kingdom • United States

Unit 0

LANGUAGE IN USE

1 **Listen.** Look and circle. **TR: 0.1**

1.

2.

3.

2 **Listen and circle.** **TR: 0.2**

1.

yes no

2.

yes no

3.

yes no

COLORS AND NUMBERS

1 **Listen.** Color and say. **TR: 0.3**

1.

2.

2 **Listen.** Color and say. **TR: 0.4**

3 **Look.** Count and write.

4 **Listen.** Draw and color. **TR: 0.5**

THE SOUNDS OF ENGLISH

1 Listen and say. TR: 0.6

2 Listen and look. Which word is different? Circle. TR: 0.7

1.

2.

3 Listen and chant. Point. TR: 0.8

Hello, hello.
Hi there, hi.

Time to go.
Bye, goodbye!

Unit 1

My School

VOCABULARY

1 **Listen.** Look and circle. **TR: 1.1**

1.

2.

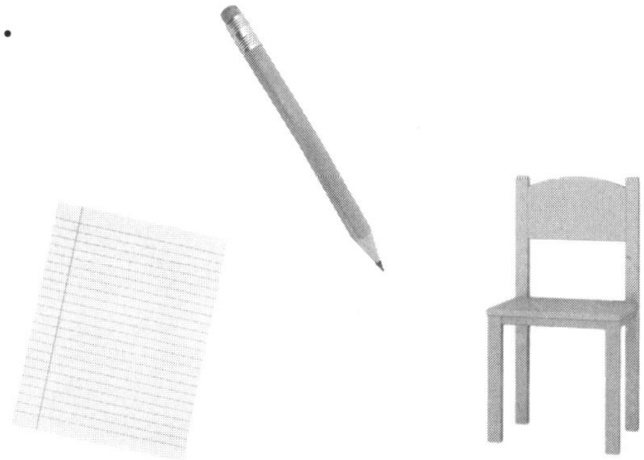

3.

4.

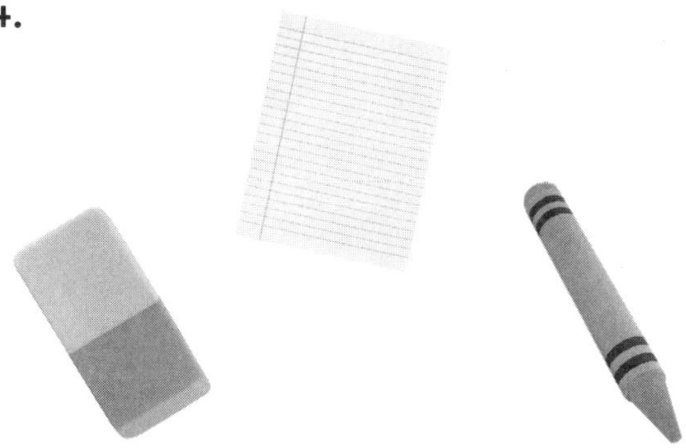

5.

6.

LANGUAGE IN USE

1 **Listen and say.** TR: 1.2

2 **Cut out the cards in the back of the workbook.**

Listen. Glue the cards. Say. TR: 1.3

1	2	3	4
5	6	7	8

3 **Match.** Say.

COLORS AND NUMBERS

1 **Listen.** Color and say. **TR: 1.4**

1. 
2. 
3. 
4. 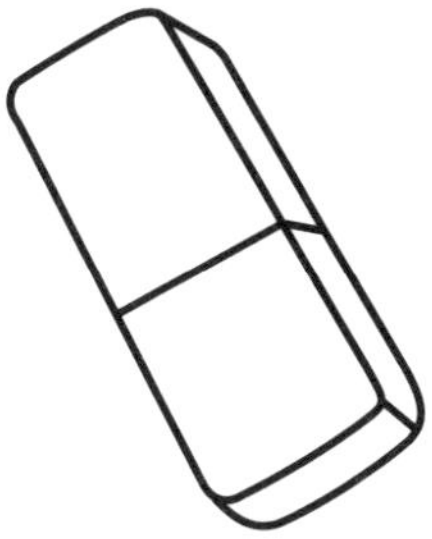

2 **Listen.** Color. Count and say. **TR: 1.5**

3 **Listen.** Count and write. **TR: 1.6**

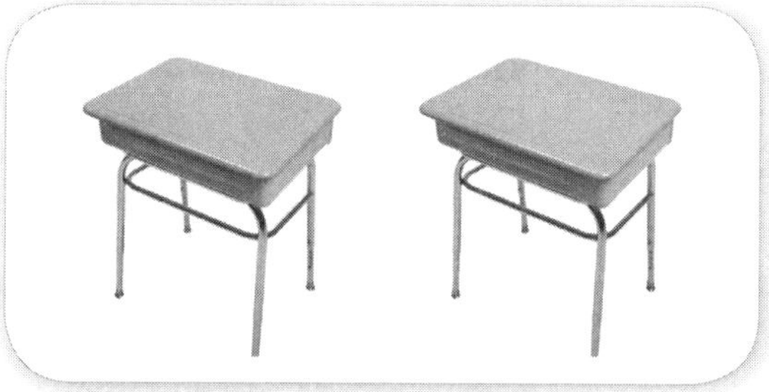

____

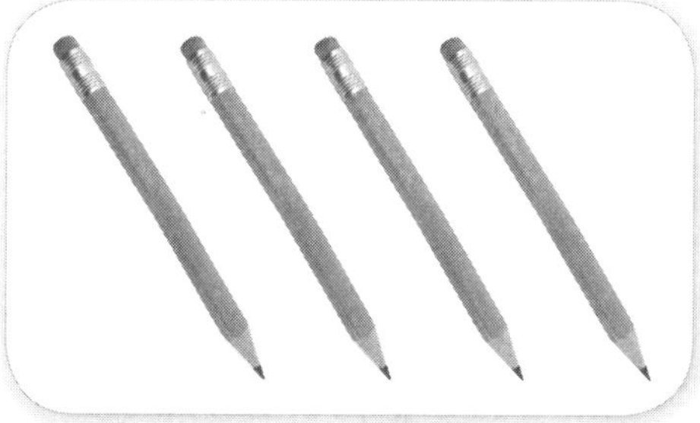

____

____

____

THE SOUNDS OF ENGLISH

1 **Listen and say.** TR: 1.7

2 **Listen and look.** Which word is different? Circle. TR: 1.8

1.

2.

3.

3 **Listen and chant.** Say a new verse. TR: 1.9

I have some 

I have a 

I have a 

Let's draw again!

I have an 

I have a 

I have some 

Let's draw again!

Unit 2

My Toys

VOCABULARY

1 **Listen.** Look and circle. **TR: 2.1**

1.

2.

3.

4.

5.

6.

LANGUAGE IN USE

1 Listen and say. **TR: 2.2**

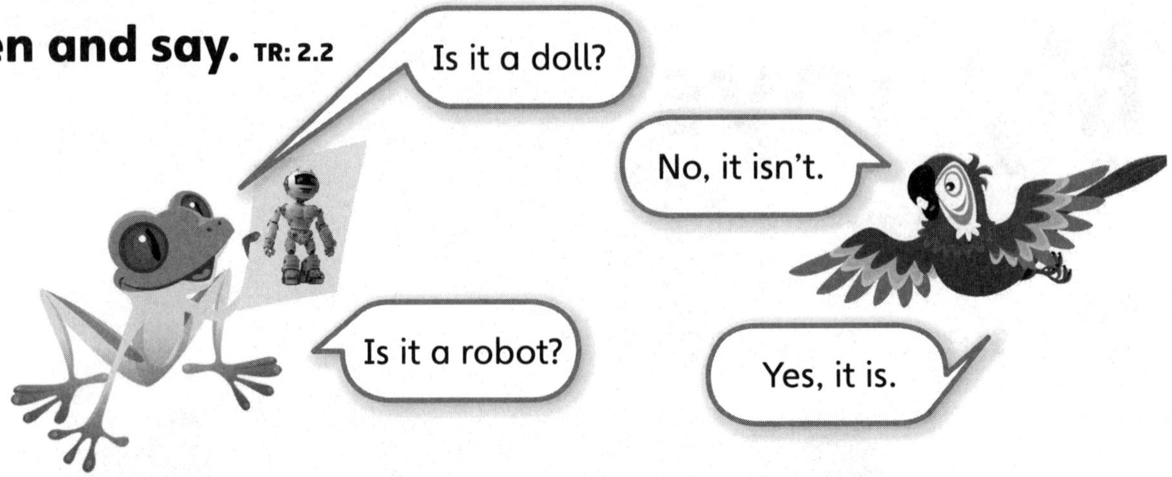

2 Cut out the cards in the back of the workbook. Listen. What is it? Glue the cards. Say. **TR: 2.3**

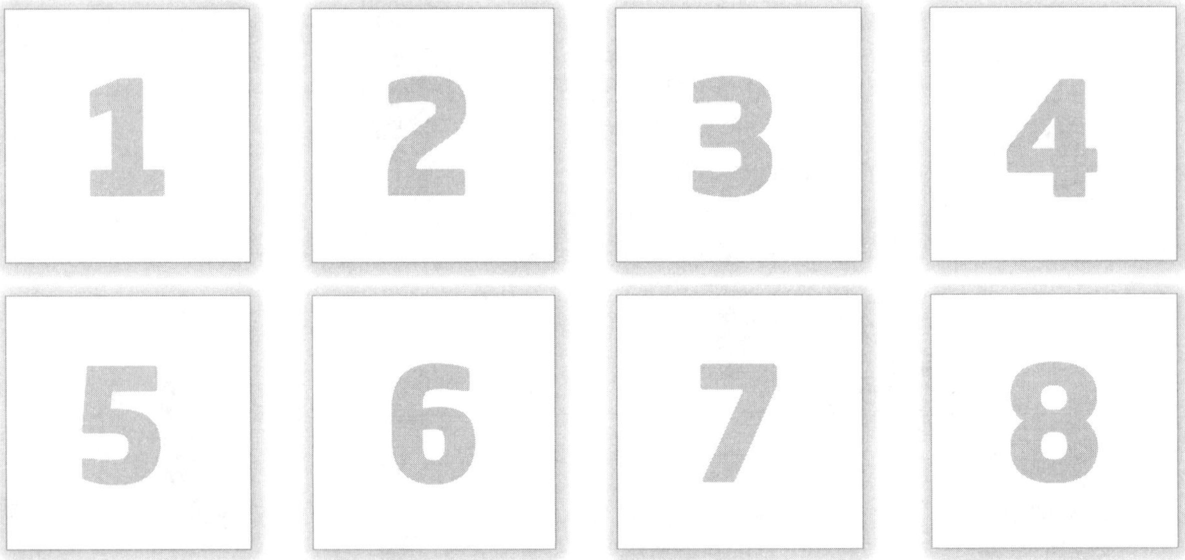

3 Draw your favorite toy. Color. What is it? Say.

COLORS AND NUMBERS

1 **Listen.** Color and say. TR: 2.4

1.

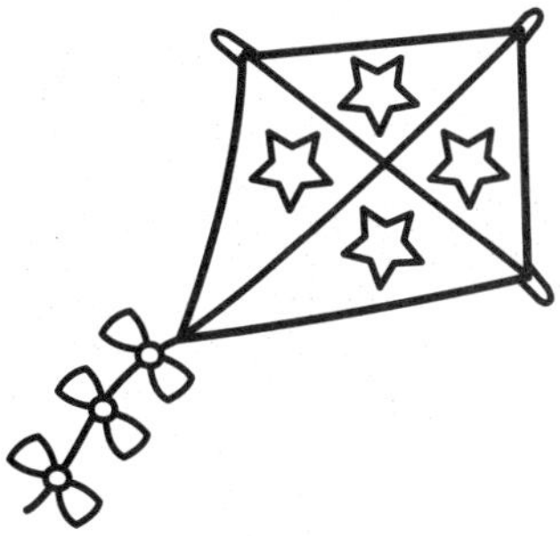

2.

3.

4.

2 **Listen.** Color. Count and say. TR: 2.5

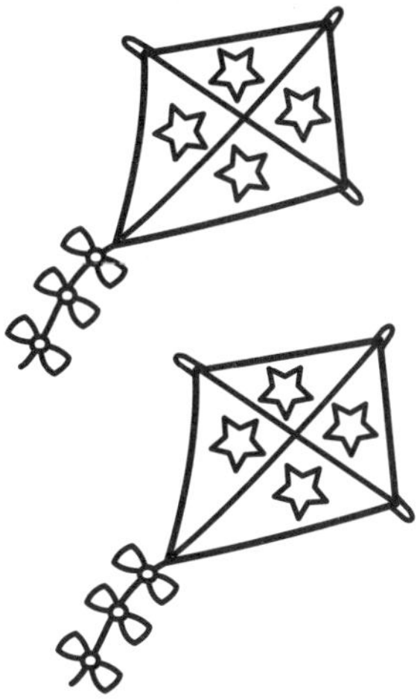

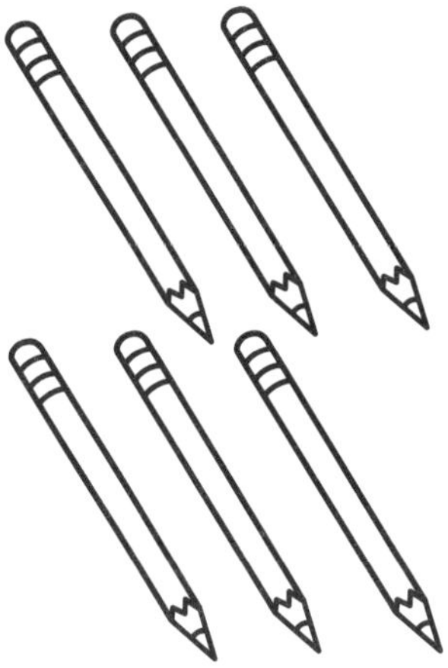

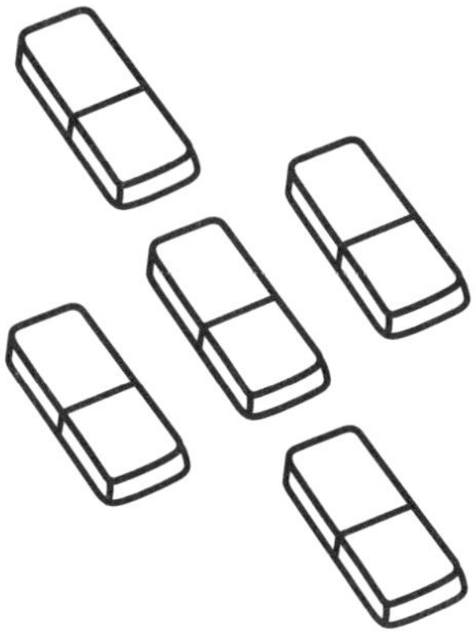

3 **Listen.** Count and write. TR: 2.6

______

______

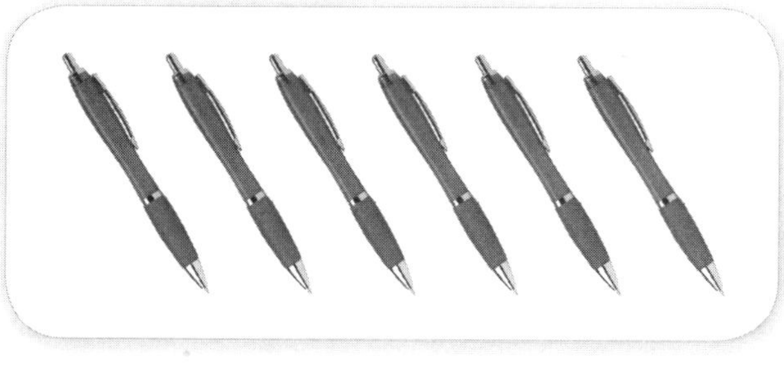

______

______

THE SOUNDS OF ENGLISH

1 **Listen and say.** TR: 2.7

2 **Listen and look.** Which word is different? Circle. TR: 2.8

I.

2.

3.

3 **Listen and chant.** Say a new verse. TR: 2.9

 and 

and more toys.

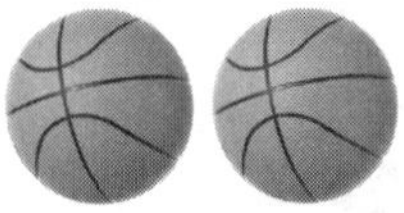 and 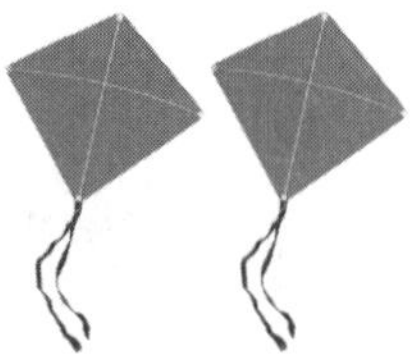

for girls and boys!

 and 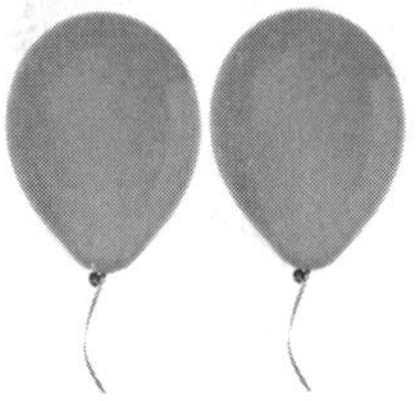

and more toys.

 and 

for girls and boys!

Unit 3

My Family

VOCABULARY

1 **Listen and look.** Draw a line. **TR: 3.1**

1

2

3

4

5

6

7

8

9

10

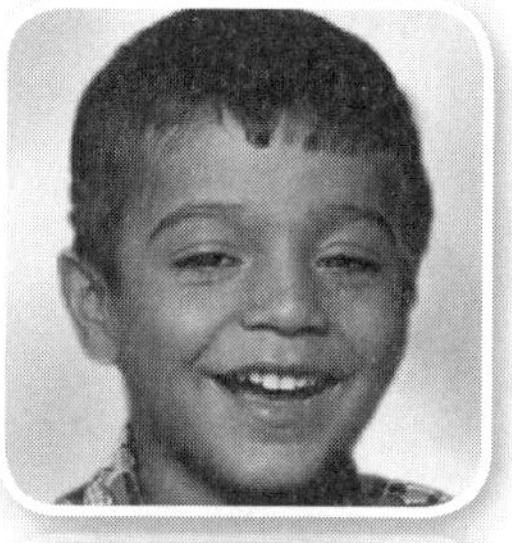

LANGUAGE IN USE

1 Listen and say. TR: 3.2

2 Listen and circle. TR: 3.3

1.

2.

3.

3 Listen and say. TR: 3.4

4 Cut out the cards in the back of the workbook. Listen. Where's the family? Glue the cards. Say. TR: 3.5

COLORS AND NUMBERS

1 **Listen.** Color and say. **TR: 3.6**

1.

2.

3.

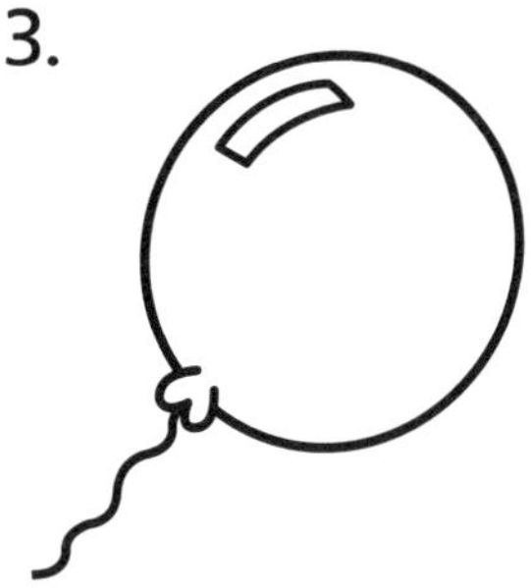

4.

2 **Listen.** Color. Count and say. **TR: 3.7**

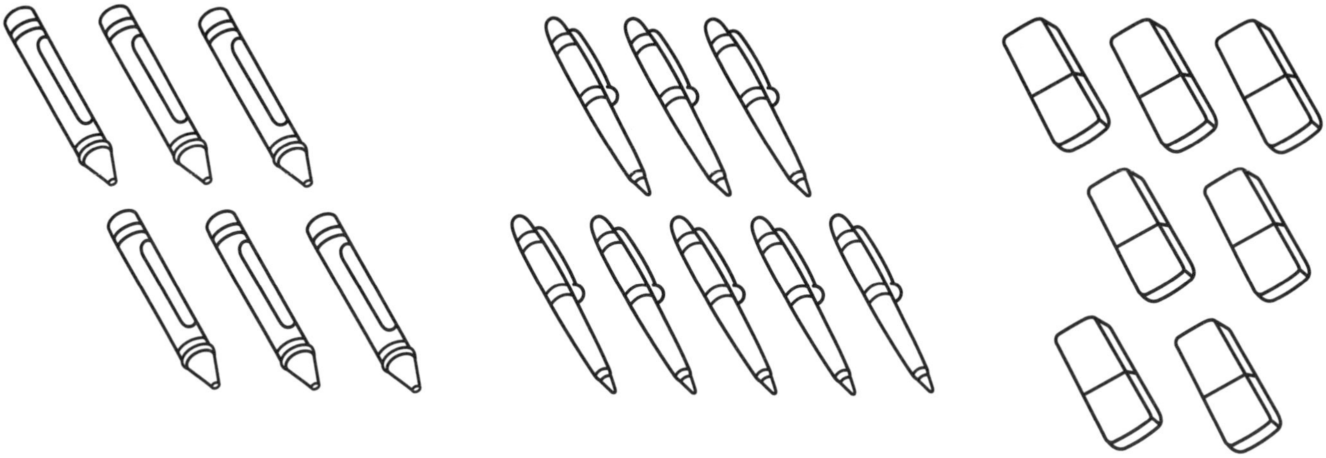

3 **Listen.** Count and write. **TR: 3.8**

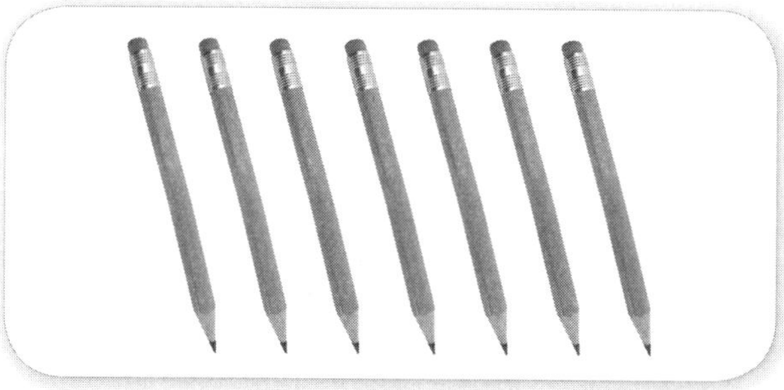

______

______

______

______

THE SOUNDS OF ENGLISH

1 Listen and say. TR: 3.9

2 Listen and look. Which word is different? Circle. TR: 3.10

1.

2.

3.

3 Listen and chant. Say a new verse. TR: 3.11

I love my 

Oh yes, I do.

My  and my 

love him, too.

I love my 

Oh yes, I do.

My  and my 

love her, too.

Unit 4

My Body

VOCABULARY

1 **Listen and look.** Draw a line. TR: 4.1

LANGUAGE IN USE

1 **Listen and say.** **TR: 4.2**

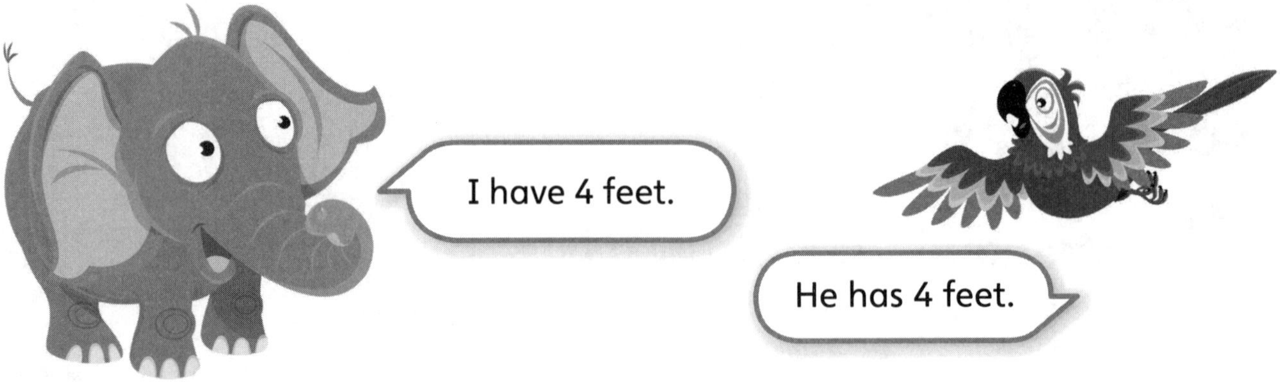

2 **Listen and circle.** Say. **TR: 4.3**

1.

2.

3.
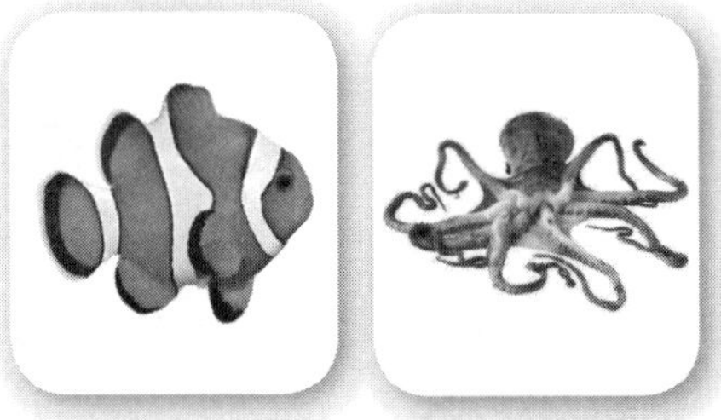

4.

3 **Cut out the cards in the back of the workbook.**
Listen and look. Glue the cards. Say. **TR: 4.4**

1	2	3	4

COLORS AND NUMBERS

1 **Listen.** Color and say. **TR: 4.5**

1.

2.

3.

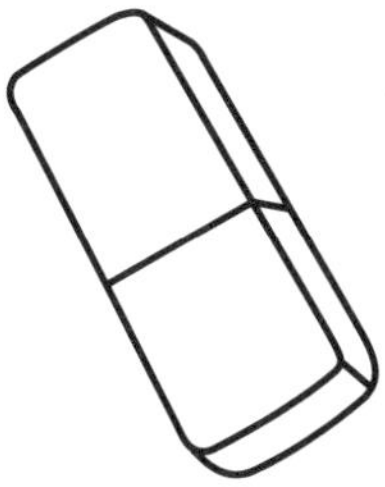

4.

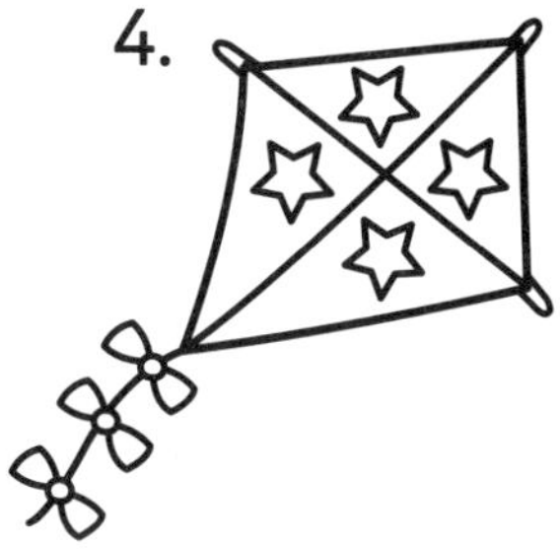

2 **Listen.** Color. Count and say. **TR: 4.6**

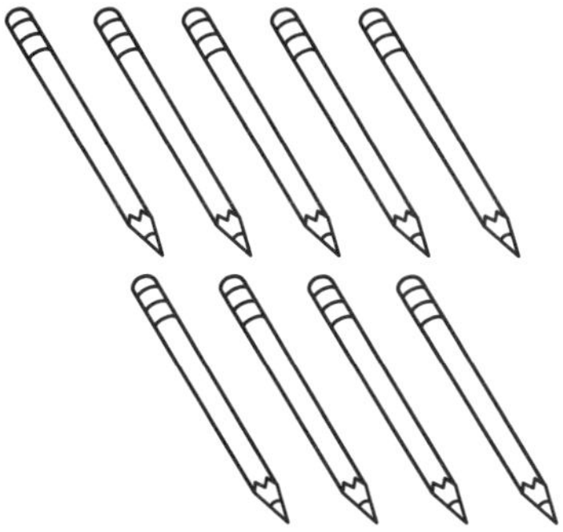

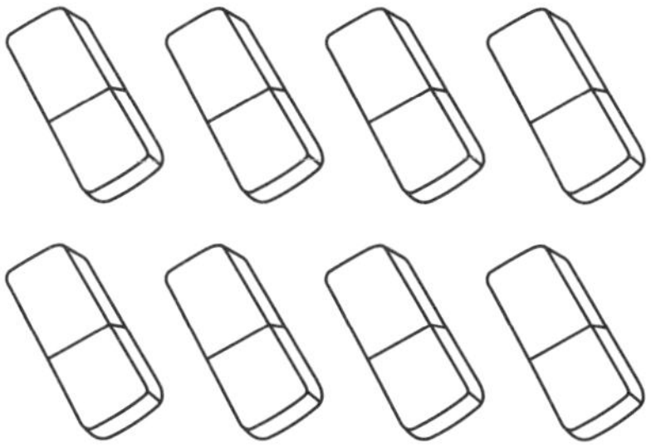

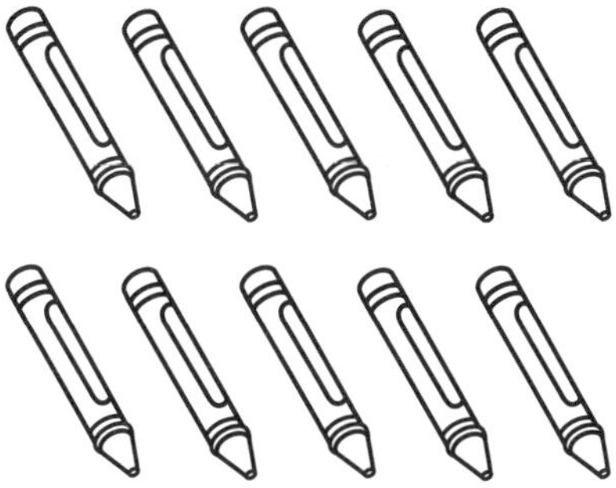

3 **Listen.** Count and write. **TR: 4.7**

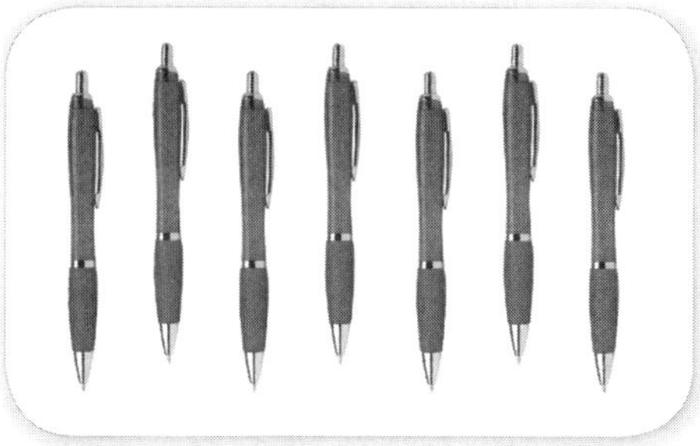

_____

_____

_____

_____

THE SOUNDS OF ENGLISH

1 **Listen and say.** TR: 4.8

2 **Listen and look.** Which word is different? Circle. TR: 4.9

1.

2.

3.

3 **Listen and chant.** Say a new verse. TR: 4.10

One 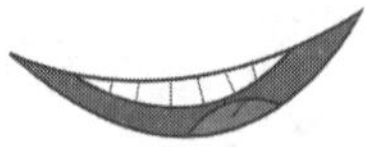 for me.

Two  for you.

Two  for me.

Two 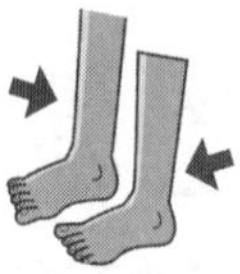 for you!

No  for me.

Brown  for you.

A  for me,

and  , too!

mustache

Units 1–4

Review

1 **Listen.** Look and circle. **TR: 4.11**

1.

2.

3.

4.

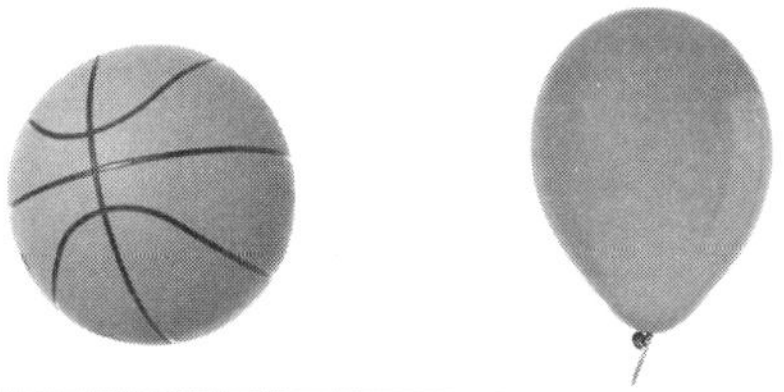

5.

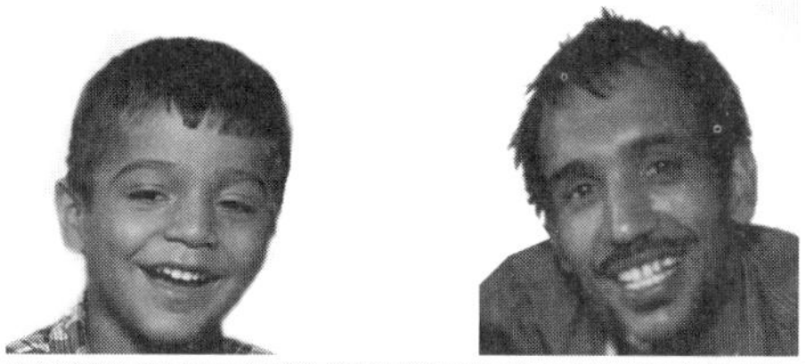

6.

7.

8.

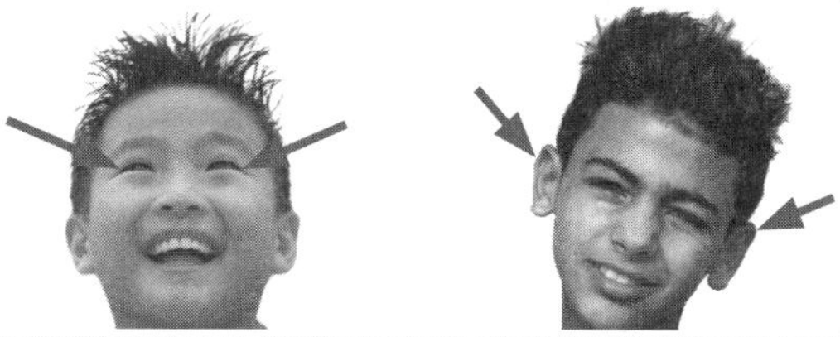

2 **Listen and color. TR: 4.12**

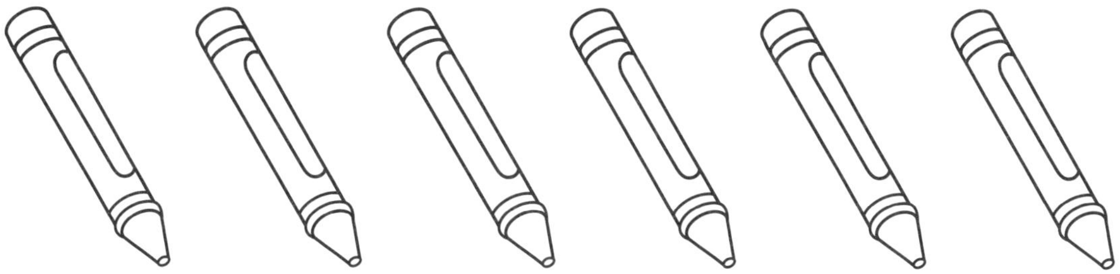

3 **Listen.** Look and circle. **TR: 4.13**

1. 

2. 

3. 

4 **Listen.** Count and circle. **TR: 4.14**

1. 

2. 

3. 

4. 

Unit 5

Stories

VOCABULARY

1 **Listen.** Look and circle. **TR: 5.1**

1.

2.

3.

4.

5.

6.

2 **Listen.** Draw. **TR: 5.2**

1.

2.

LANGUAGE IN USE

1 **Listen and say.** TR: 5.3

2 **Cut out the cards in the back of the workbook.** Listen. Glue the cards. Say. TR: 5.4

1	2	3	4
5	6	7	8

3 **Draw.** What do you want? Say. Color.

COLORS

1 **Listen.** Color and say. **TR: 5.5**

1.

2.

3.

4.

2 **Listen.** Color. Count and say. **TR: 5.6**

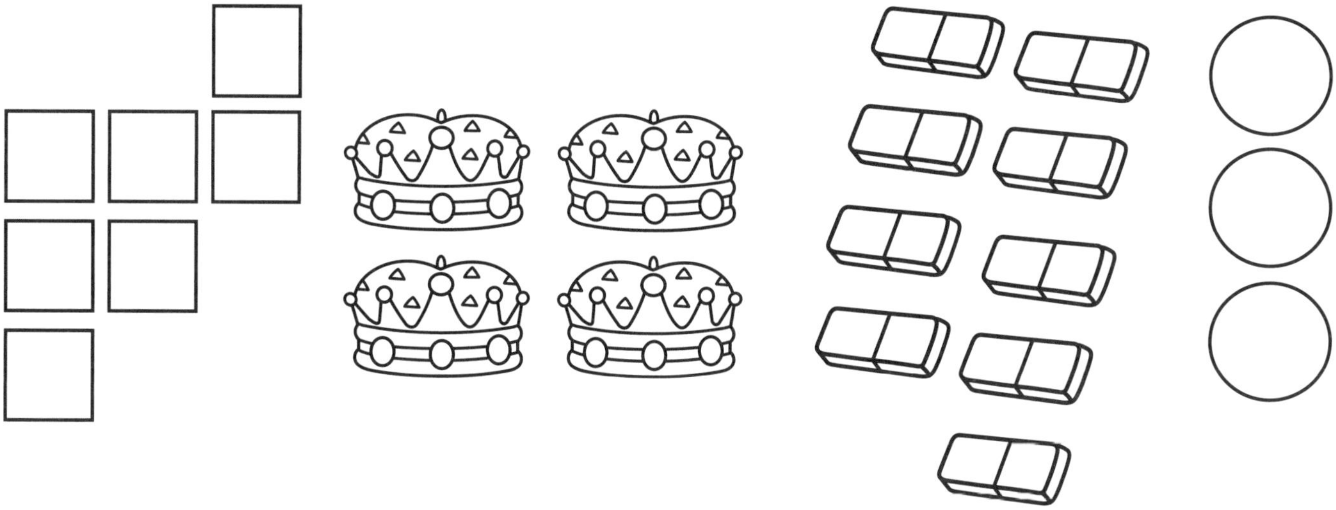

3 **Listen.** Count and write. **TR: 5.7**

______

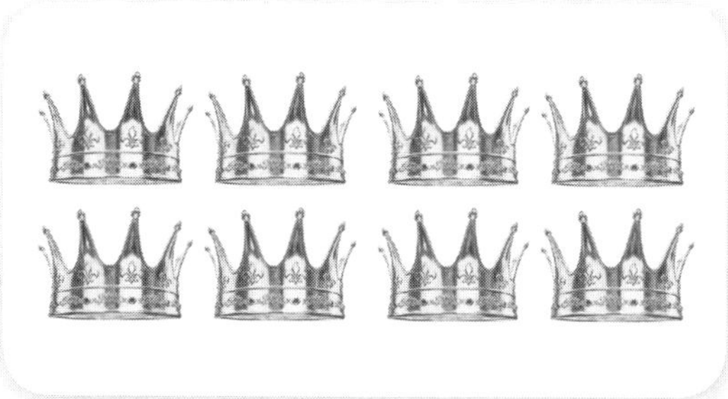

______

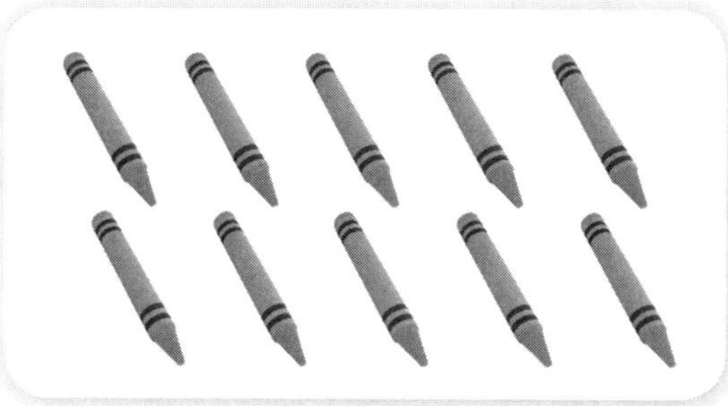

______

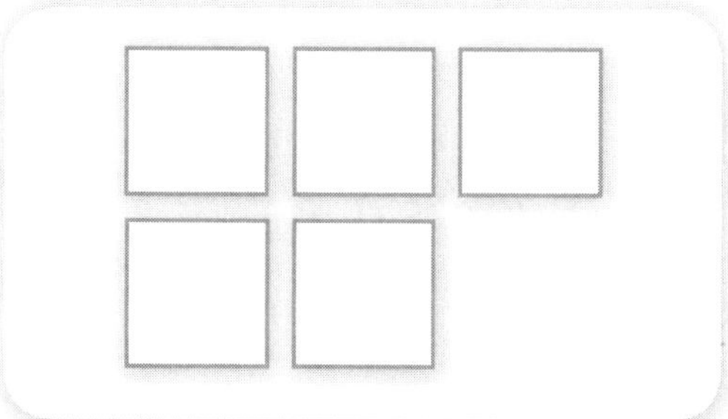

______

THE SOUNDS OF ENGLISH

1 **Listen and say.** **TR: 5.8**

2 **Listen and look.** Which word is different? Circle. **TR: 5.9**

1.   

2.   

3.   

3 **Listen and chant.** Say a new verse. **TR: 5.10**

The  wants silver.

The  wants gold.

The  wants a  of silver *and* gold!

The  wants silver.

The  wants gold.

The  wants a 

of silver *and* gold!

Unit 6

I Like Food

VOCABULARY

1 **Listen.** Look and circle. **TR: 6.1**

1.

2.

3.

4.

5.

6.

LANGUAGE IN USE

1 Listen and say. **TR: 6.2**

2 Cut out the cards in the back of the workbook.
Glue the cards. Say.

I like . . .	I don't like . . .

3 What is your favorite food? Draw.

SHAPES

1 **Listen and color.** Listen, count, and say. **TR: 6.3**

1.

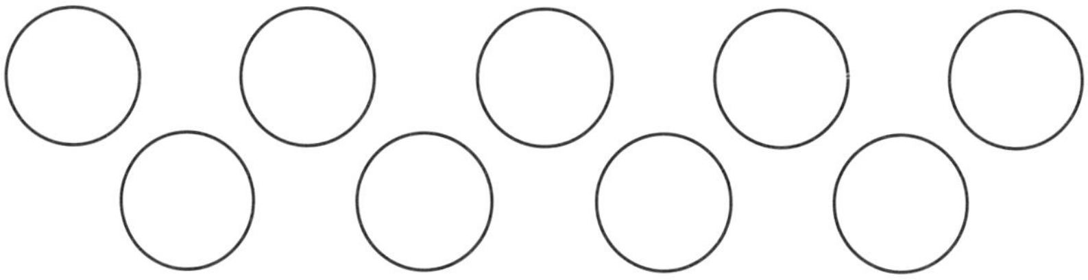

2.

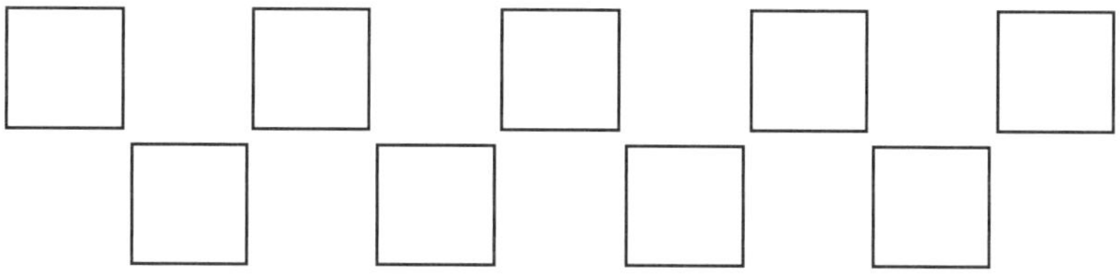

2 **Count and say.** How many circles? How many squares?

circles ____

squares ____

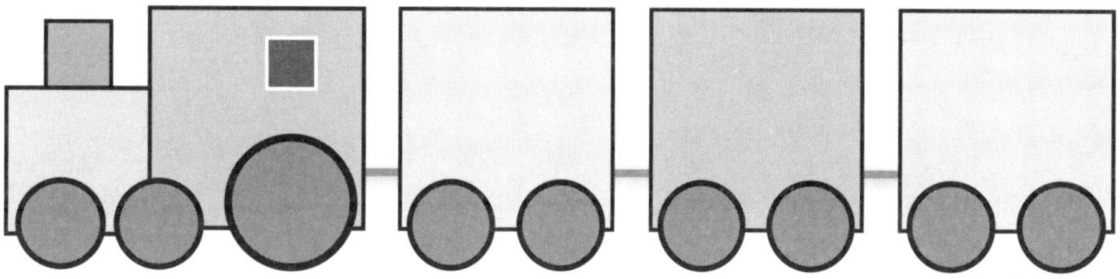

3 **Listen.** Count and say. **TR: 6.4**

 ____

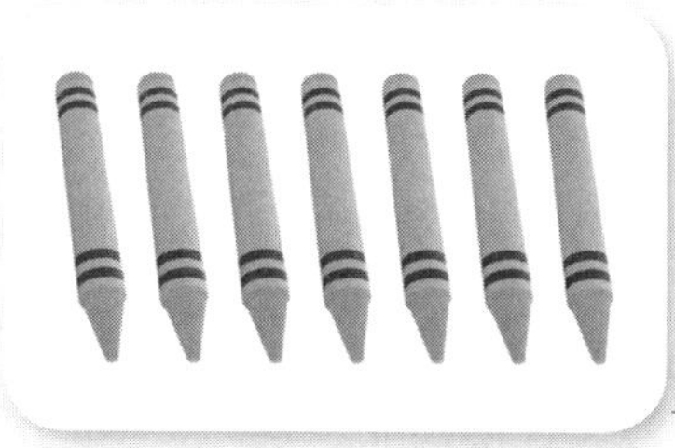 ____

 ____

 ____

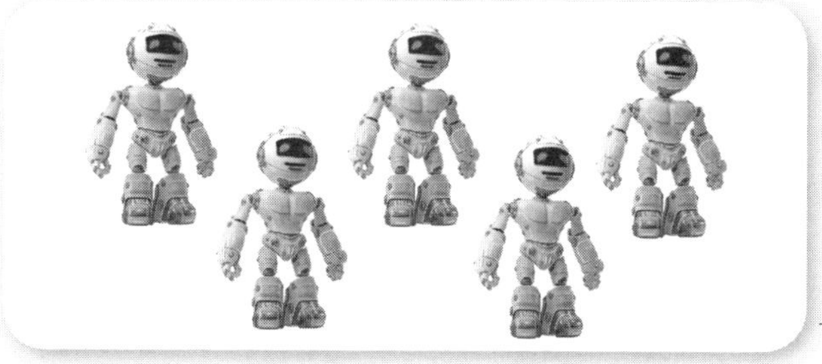 ____

THE SOUNDS OF ENGLISH

1 **Listen and say.** TR: 6.5

2 **Listen and look.** Which word is different? Circle. TR: 6.6

1.

2.

  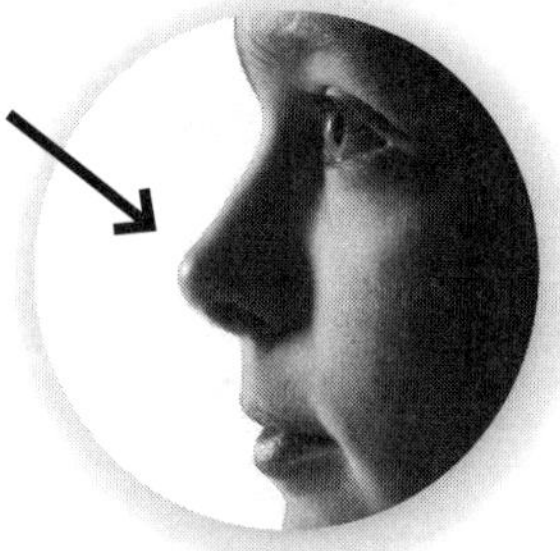

3.

3 **Listen and chant.** Say a new verse. TR: 6.7

I like 

I like 

I like 

They're so nice!

I like 

I like 

I like 

They're so nice!

Unit 7

Clothes

VOCABULARY

1 **Listen and look.** Draw a line. **TR: 7.1**

1
2
3
4
5
6
7
8

2 **Listen and look.** Circle and color. **TR: 7.2**

LANGUAGE IN USE

1 Listen and say. TR: 7.3

It's hot. I'm wearing shorts.

It's cold. He's wearing a hat.

2 Cut out the cards in the back of the workbook.

Listen. Glue the cards. Say. TR: 7.4

1	2	3	4
5	6	7	8

3 Connect the dots. What is it? Say. Color.

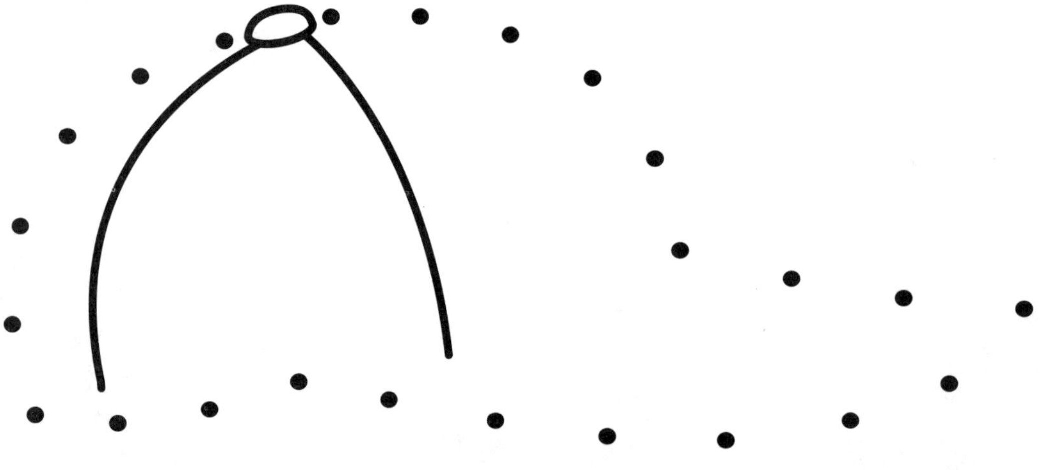

SHAPES

1 **Listen.** Color and say. **TR: 7.5**

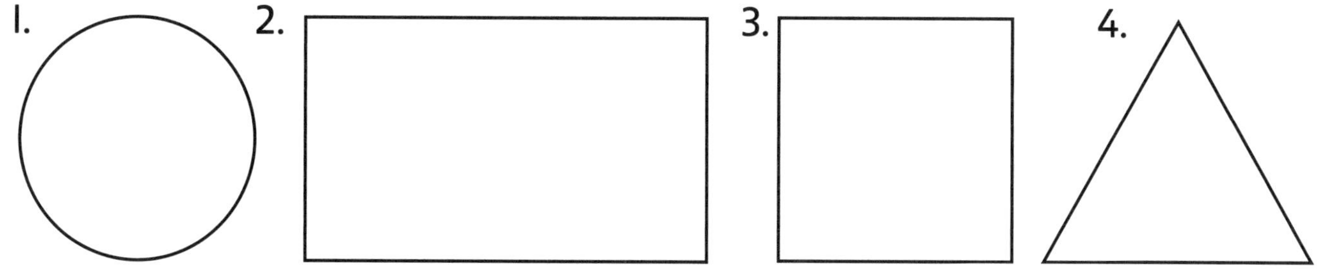

2 **Listen.** Color. Count and say. **TR: 7.6**

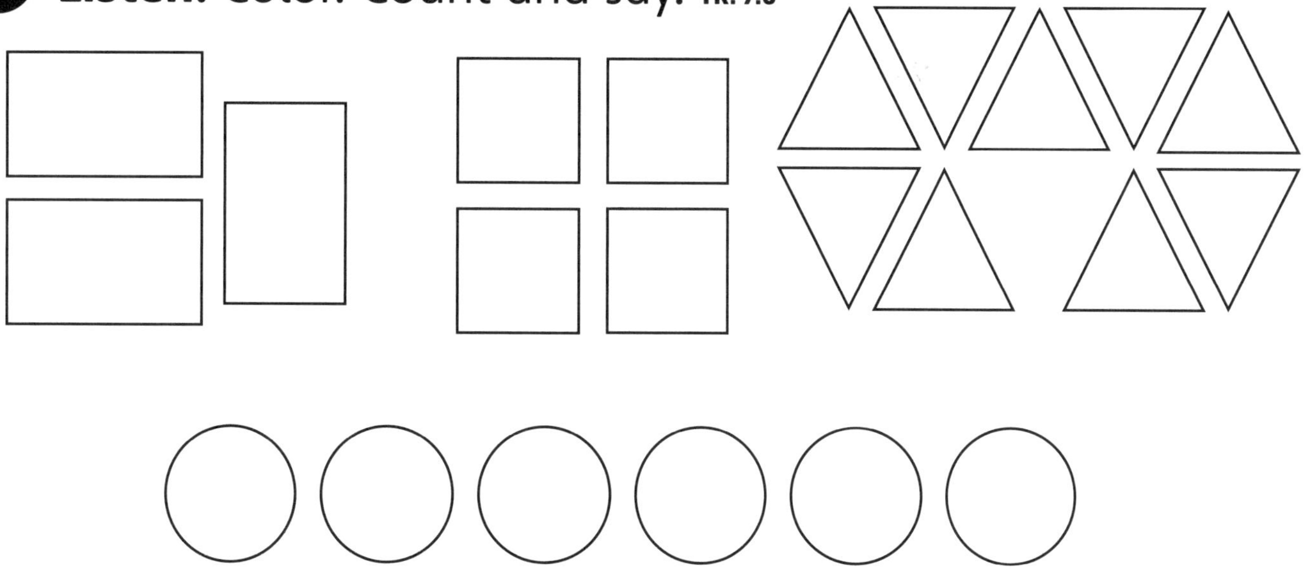

3 **Listen.** Count and write. **TR: 7.7**

______

______

______

______

THE SOUNDS OF ENGLISH

1 **Listen and say.** **TR: 7.8**

2 **Listen and look.** Which word is different? Circle. **TR: 7.9**

1.

2.

3.

3 **Listen and chant.** Say a new verse. **TR: 7.10**

I want a 

My sister wants a 

Let's shop for clothes.

 please say yes!

I want some 

My sister wants a 

We want new clothes.

 please say yes!

Unit 8

Animals

VOCABULARY

1 **Listen and look.** Draw a line. **TR: 8.1**

1
2
3
4
5
6
7
8
9
10

LANGUAGE IN USE

1 **Listen and say.** TR: 8.2

2 **Cut out the cards in the back of the workbook.**
Listen. Glue the cards. Say. TR: 8.3

1	2	3	4
5	6	7	8

3 **Connect the dots.** What is it? Say. Color.

SHAPES

1 **Listen.** Color and say. **TR: 8.4**

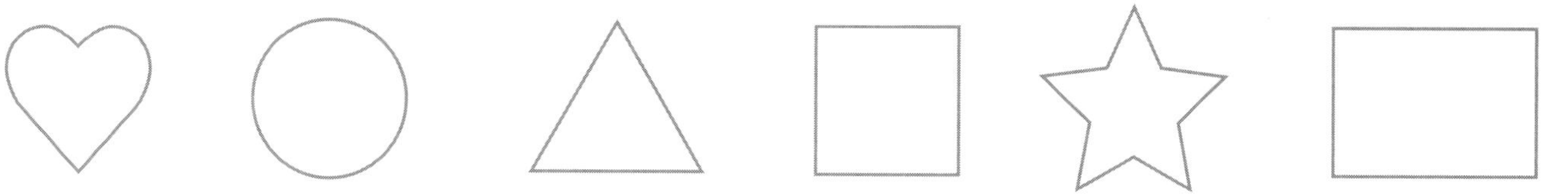

2 **Listen.** Color. Count and say. **TR: 8.5**

3 **Listen.** Count and write. **TR: 8.6**

______

______

______

______

THE SOUNDS OF ENGLISH

1 **Listen and say.** TR: 8.7

2 **Listen and look.** Which word is different? Circle. TR: 8.8

1.

2.

3.

3 **Listen and chant.** Say a new verse. TR: 8.9

Look, I'm a
I walk and I run.

Look, I'm a
standing in the sun.

Look, I'm a
I walk and I run.

Look, I'm a
standing in the sun.

Units 5–8

Review

1 **Listen.** Look and circle. **TR: 8.10**

1.

2.

3.

4.

5.

6.

7.

8.

2 **Listen.** Look and circle. **TR: 8.11**

1.

2.

3.

3 **Listen and color.** **TR: 8.12**

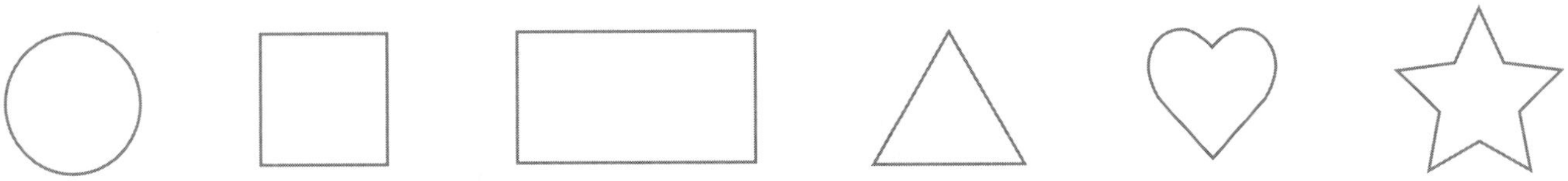

4 **Listen.** Count and circle. **TR: 8.13**

1.
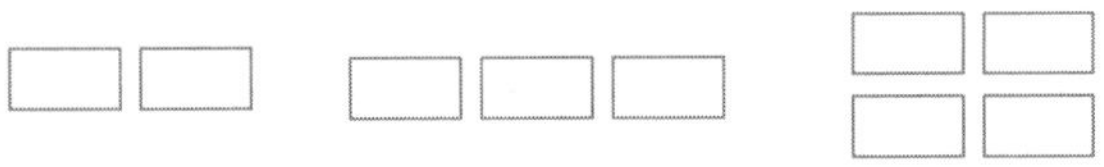

2.

3.

4.
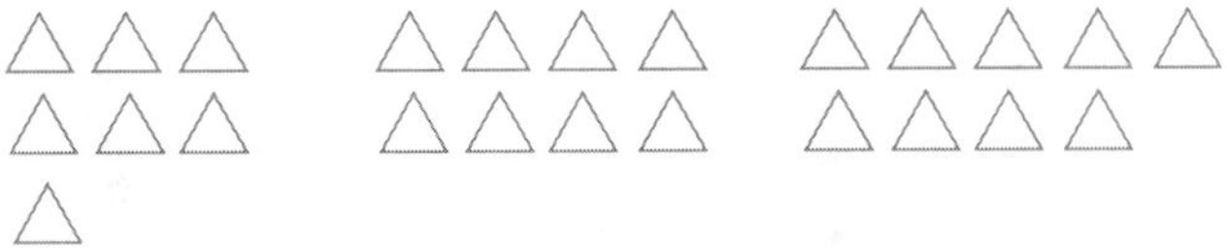

5.
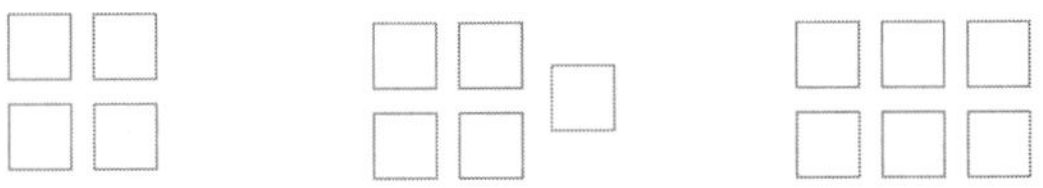

6.

Trace and write. Use with **Unit 1.**

a a a

A A A

b b b

B B B

apple

paper

book

bye

Trace and write.

Use with **Unit 1.**

c c c

C C C

1 1 1 2 2 2

3 3 3 4 4 4

crayon

pencil

chair

car

Trace and write.

Use with **Unit 2.**

d d d

D D D

e e e

E E E

pen

desk

teddy bear

Trace and write.

Use with **Unit 2.**

f f f

F F F

5 5 5

6 6 6

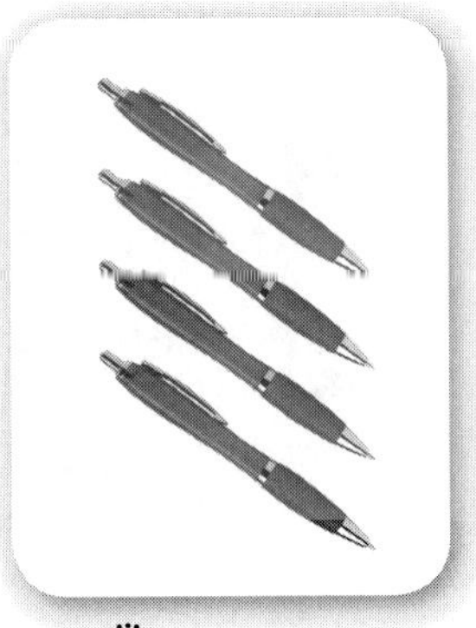

four

eraser

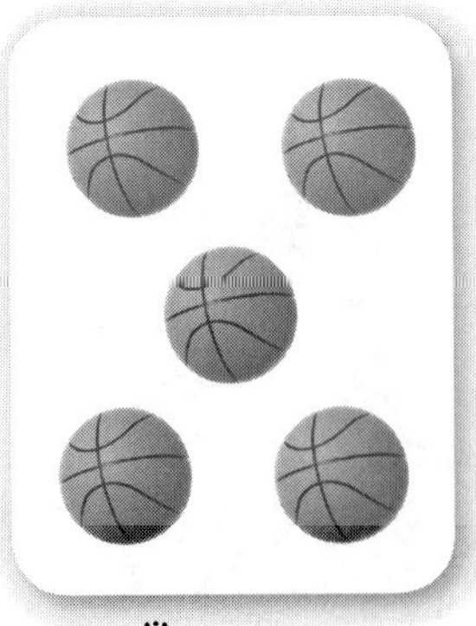

five

Trace and write.

Use with **Unit 3.**

g g g

G G G

h h h

H H H

father

mother

grandma

hello

Trace and write.

Use with **Unit 3.**

i i i

I I I

7 7 7

8 8 8

sisters

pencil

Mia

Eddie

Trace and write.

Use with **Unit 4.**

j j j

J J J

k k k

K K K

kite

kitchen

juice

truck

Trace and write.

Use with **Unit 4.**

l l l

L L L

9 9 9

10 10 10

ball

balloon

doll

living room

Trace and write.

Use with **Unit 5.**

m m m

M M M

n n n

N N N

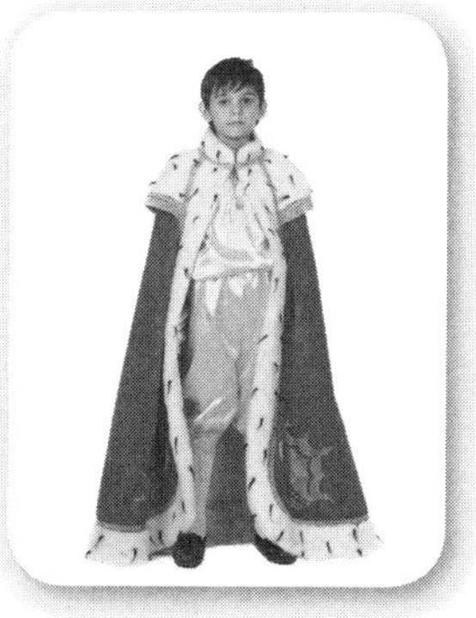

prince

grandma

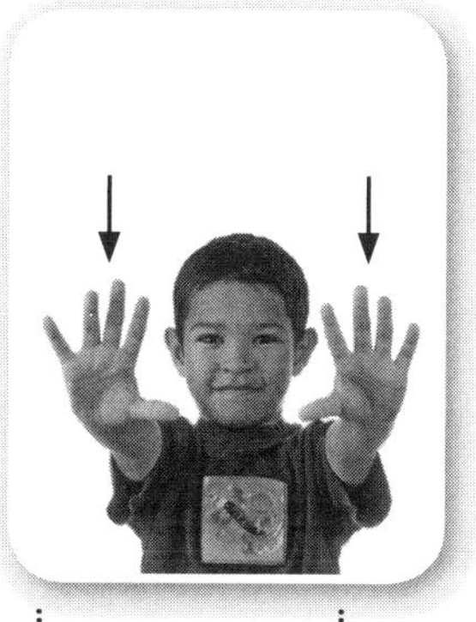

hands

friends

Trace and write.

o o o

O O O

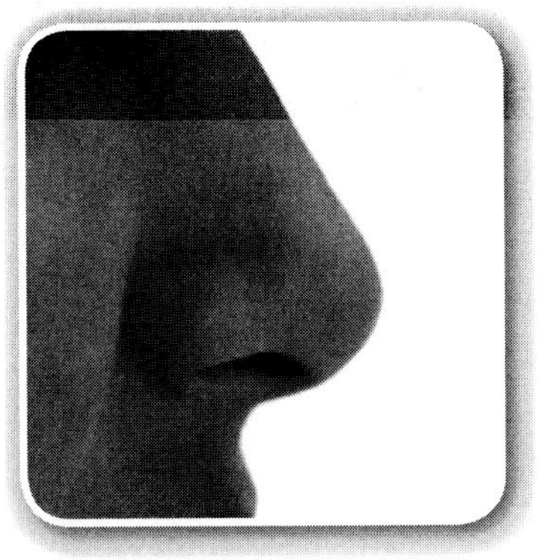

nose

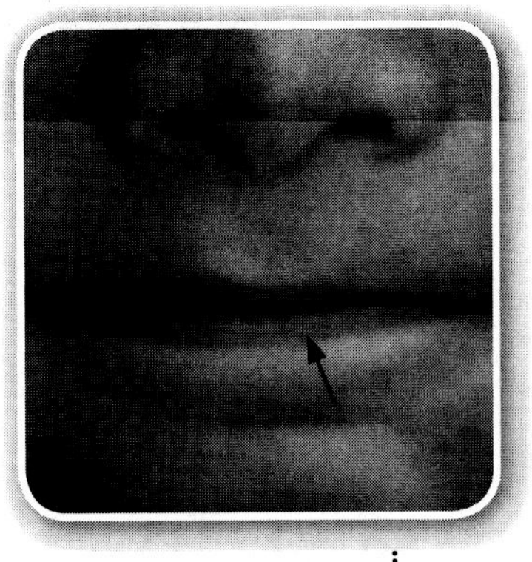

mouth

balloon

bathroom

robot

book

Trace and write.

Use with **Unit 6.**

p p p

P P P

q q q

Q Q Q

pen

queen

pencil

paper

Trace and write.

Use with **Unit 6.**

r r r

R R R

grandpa

car

rice

prince

bread

crown

Trace and write.

s s s

S S S

t t t

T T T

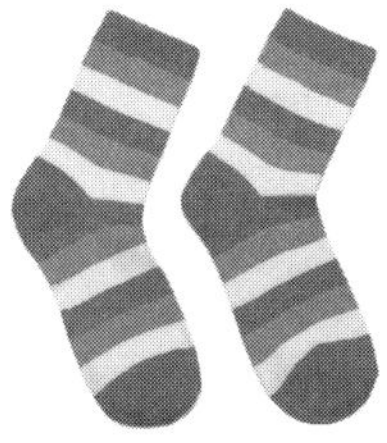

socks

shorts

skirt

shirt

Trace and write.

Use with **Unit 7.**

u u u

U U U

v v v

V V V

Write your name.

Trace and write.

Use with **Unit 8.**

w w w

W W W

x x x

X X X

? ? ?

! ! !

Trace and write.

Use with **Unit 8.**

y y y

Y Y Y

z z z

Z Z Z

Do you like school?

Yes, I do!

Unit 1 Cutouts   Use with **LANGUAGE IN USE** Activity 2.

Unit 2 Cutouts   Use with **LANGUAGE IN USE** Activity 2.

Unit 3 Cutouts Use with **LANGUAGE IN USE** Activity 4.

Unit 4 Cutouts Use with **LANGUAGE IN USE** Activity 3.

Unit 5 Cutouts Use with **LANGUAGE IN USE** Activity 2.

Unit 6 Cutouts Use with **LANGUAGE IN USE** Activity 2.

Unit 7 Cutouts Use with **LANGUAGE IN USE** Activity 2.

Unit 8 Cutouts Use with **LANGUAGE IN USE** Activity 2.